I don't like the dark

First published in this edition in 2010 by Evans Brothers Ltd
2A Portman Mansions
Chiltern Street
London W1U 6NR

This edition © Evans Brothers Limited 2010
© Van In, Lier, 1995. Van In Publishers, Grote Markt 39, 2500 Lier, Belgium

Originally published in Belgium as Mag het licht nog even ann?

British Library Cataloguing in Publication Data

Bode, Ann de.
   I don't like the dark. -- (Side by side)
   1. Fear of the dark--Juvenile fiction. 2. Cousins--
Juvenile fiction. 3. Children's stories.
   I. Title II. Series
   839.3'1364-dc22

ISBN-13: 9780237543068

Printed in China

Kate is going to stay with
her cousin, Sophie.
She waves goodbye to Mum.
'Be good,' says Mum.
'See you soon!'

At Sophie's, the girls chatter.
'I've brought you a present,' says Kate,
looking in her case.
Zebbie the zebra is sitting on the top.
I won't give *him* away! thinks Kate.

Kate rummages through the case.
What a mess!
Things land everywhere –
even on Sophie!

'Here they are!' cries Kate.
'Right at the bottom!'
But Kate can't remember which is for
Sophie, and which is for her Auntie Julie.

They both unwrap their presents.
'Thank you, Kate,' they chorus.
Chocolates for Auntie Julie, soap for Sophie.
Hey, that's not right! So they swap.

Pancakes for tea, yummy.
Kate eats lots.
'Oof, I feel as fat as a balloon,' she laughs.

8

'Can we go to bed now?' asks Sophie.
'It's a bit early for bed, go and play for
a bit,' says her mum.
The girls are disappointed – they wanted
to play in bed!

At last, it's bedtime.
But when Kate is getting ready, she thinks about later, when it gets dark.
She is afraid of the dark.

'Let's make a tent on my bed,'
says Sophie.
The two girls tell each other
silly camping stories.

Then the tent bed turns into a boat bed.
A storm rolls in.
'Help,' cries Kate. 'We're sinking –
and the sharks will eat us up!'

So they turn the bed into a plane.
They pretend they are rescuing people.
Then the plane loses an engine,
so they jump out and back onto the bed.

'Let's be acrobats!'
'Yes, let's see how high we can jump!'
Auntie Julie calls up the stairs.
'Hey, you two, time to settle down.'

Kate snuggles down in Sophie's bed.
I don't want to be alone in the dark in
my own room, she thinks. Sophie won't
understand, she's not afraid of anything!

When they hear Auntie Julie coming upstairs, they hide under the bed. 'I can see you!' says Auntie Julie.

'Come along, Kate, time for your
own bed now.'
Kate goes very quiet.
She is worried about the dark.

As soon as she settles down on her own,
she feels afraid. She holds Zebbie tightly,
trying to stop the monsters coming.

Perhaps they are under the bed?
'Can you *see* anything, Zebbie?'
she whispers.

As soon as she lies down again, she sees it – a monster with several heads is clawing its way across the wall towards her.

Aaaagh! Now there's a black ghost,
and bat shapes.
Go away! Go away!

Kate closes her eyes very tight.
I wish I was at home with Mum, she thinks.
I wish I was big and strong and not afraid.
If I wake Sophie she'll just make fun of me.

At last Kate falls asleep.
But she has a scary dream about sharks
with sharp teeth, and wakes up.

She creeps out of bed and gets her
torch out of her case.
What was that? A noise on the stairs!

The door opens slowly.
Kate switches on her torch.
It lights up her face.
'Aaagh! Help, a ghost!' cries Auntie Julie.

'It's me, not a ghost,' says Kate.
'So it is, silly me,' says her auntie,
laughing nervously.

The noise wakes Sophie up.
Auntie Julie tells the girls about her ghost,
and Kate tells the others
about her scary monsters.
She feels better
having told them.

'Look, Kate, your monster was the shadow
of that big tree moving in the wind.'
Kate still feels afraid of the dark, though.
'Could you leave the light on please, Auntie?'

'Of course. It's the best way to keep ghosts away! You're very brave, you know,' says Auntie Julie. 'You have to be very brave to admit that you're scared.'

The next day the cousins draw lots of monsters. Not frightening monsters, just funny ones. I'll try to laugh if I see any monsters in bed tonight, thinks Kate bravely.

Suddenly Sophie shrieks.
What's the matter? Surely she's
not afraid of that little spider?
But she is.

Kate puts the spider gently
outside the window.
'Not afraid of anything, eh?' laughs Kate.
'Well, er... perhaps just spiders, and....'
Kate smiles. Now they can *be* good
friends again.